Hidden Hope

How a Toy and a Hero Saved Lives During the Holocaust

Written by
ELISA BOXER

Illustrated by
AMY JUNE BATES

Hidden Hope

How a Toy and a Hero Saved Lives During the Holocaust

Abrams Books for Young Readers • New York

For the six million
—E.B.

To every child who thinks that they are
too small, too weak, or not brave enough
to make a difference
—A.J.B.

During the Second World War,
the first priority for Jewish people
was staying out of sight.

Because during the Second World War,
the first priority for Nazis
was getting rid of Jewish people.

And the soldiers saluted—
ready to round up and take away
anyone Jewish.

The Star of David was
a point of pride and faith.
But the Nazis turned it into a tool of hate
when they forced Jewish people
to wear badges with that star
and carry papers stamped **JUIVE**—
the French word for "Jew."

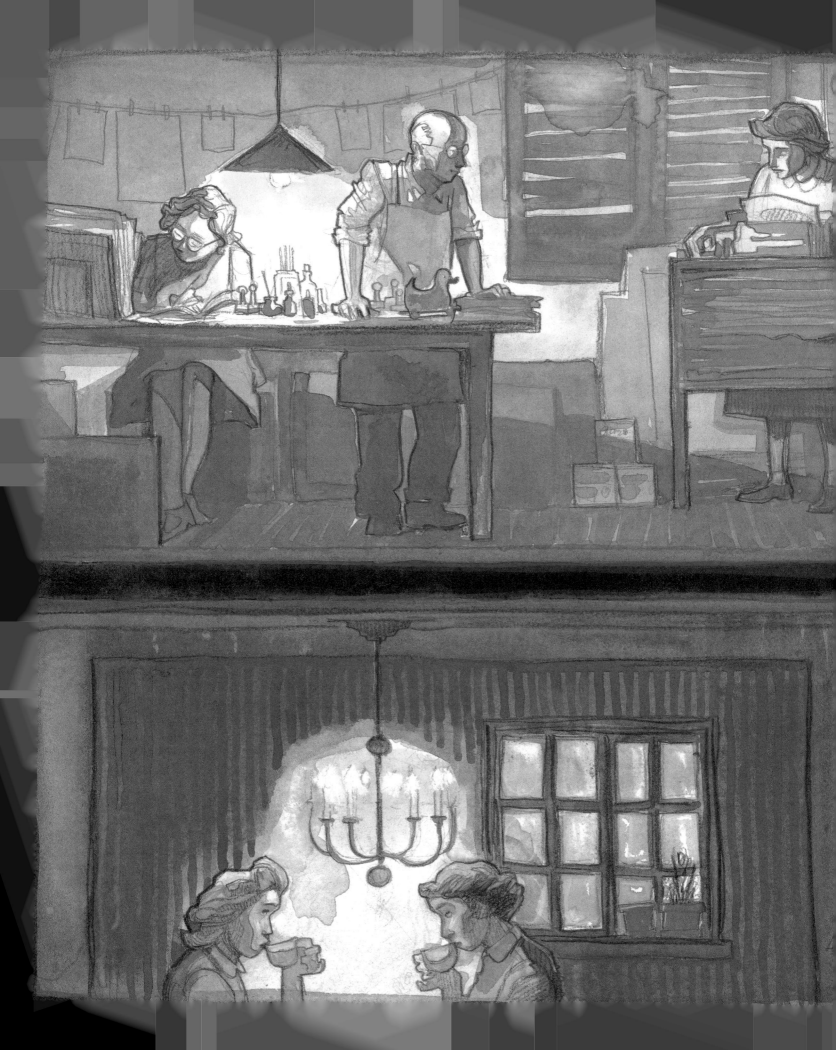

But hate has a way
of bringing out heroes.

Some brave souls dared to help.
In secret workshops,
they toiled through the night—
examining,
erasing,
fixing,
forging . . .
new papers,
new names.

Nazis barged into
homes, schools, offices, and shops,
demanding documents.
Any adult or child identified as Jewish
was immediately taken away.

But how to get those life-saving papers
to people who needed them?

There were many ways:
tucked inside books,
slipped inside shoes,
sewn inside clothes . . .

And then there was a toy.

After all, who would suspect
that a wooden duck
with an orange beak
and wheels
and wings
had a secret?

A hidden compartment.
Hope in a hollow.

But the toy couldn't
do it alone.

Jacqueline Gauthier was a teenager
at the time of the war.
She worked for the French Resistance,
a courageous network
that fought the Nazis
and protected Jewish families.

When the Nazis weren't looking,
Jacqueline slipped into those workshops
and tucked new papers into
the duck's secret chamber.

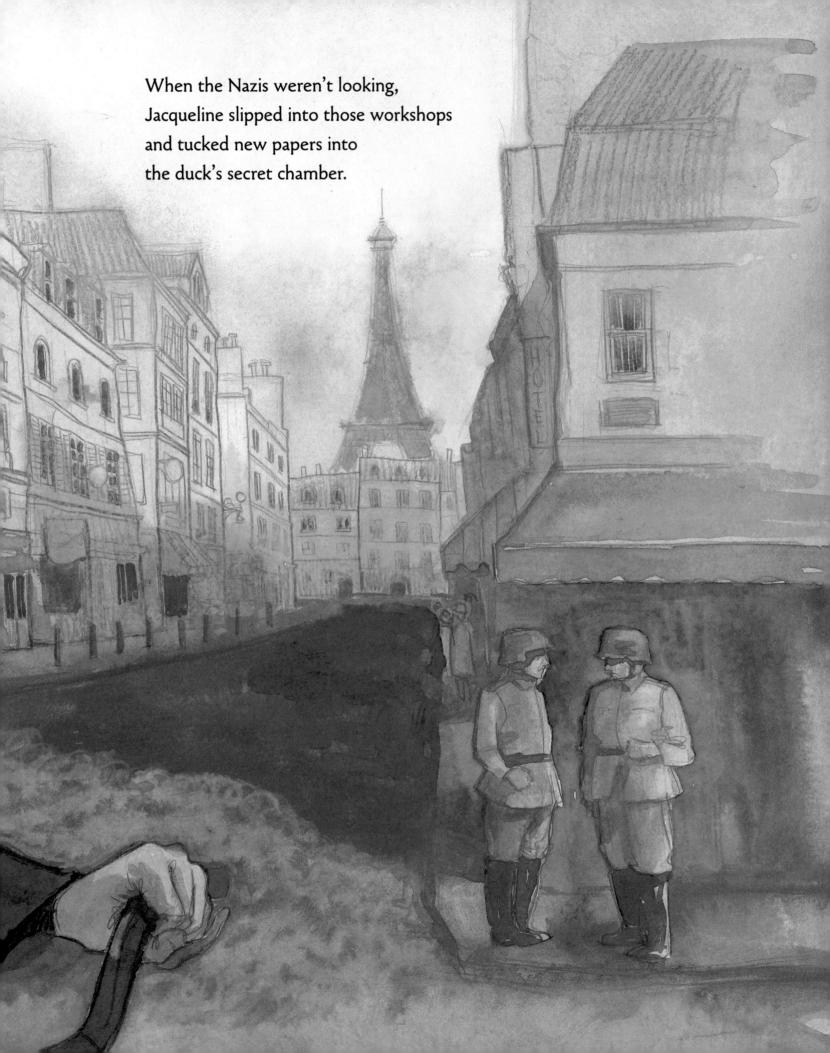

Bump, bump, bump
went her bike over the
cobblestone streets of Paris.
Racing against time,
hurrying against hate.

False papers with
new names gave people
a greater chance
of surviving the war.

If they wanted more protection,
the French Resistance provided safe passage
across the border from France into Spain,

where people could live
and learn
and play
and pray
free from capture.

No one could believe the bravery of this stranger,
Jacqueline Gauthier.
She wasn't even Jewish
and she was risking her life
to save theirs.

But the duck wasn't
Jacqueline's only secret.
She was hiding something else:
her name.
It wasn't really Jacqueline Gauthier.
It was Judith Geller.

She, in fact, *was* Jewish.
She'd found a hiding place
for her parents and brother
while she set out on her secret missions
with her own paper,
showing a pretend name.

Her document declared her
a Christian social worker
whose job was to help children.
So no one questioned why
she went into homes with a toy.
After all, who would suspect
that a wooden duck
with an orange beak
and wheels
and wings
hid such a deep secret?

Together they travelled
from one family to the next,
delivering life
by hiding the truth.

Jacqueline feared being caught.
Still, she rode on,
the duck bouncing against
the bottom of her satchel,
secrets tucked safely inside.

And then, one day . . .

"*HALT!*"

A Nazi soldier jumped out of his truck, demanding that she hand over her satchel!

She'd been caught.
She knew he'd find the duck.
Her secret missions were over.
She was afraid her life would be, too.

The Nazi opened the satchel.
He saw the duck.
He grabbed it,
yanked it out,
and yelled at Jacqueline
for wasting his time with a toy.

He stormed off to his truck
and sped away.

Heart racing, she held the
duck to her chest.
It was getting too dangerous.

But Jacqueline kept going.

Riding,

resisting,

rescuing.

Together, she and the toy duck saved more than two hundred lives.

And then came the day
Allied soldiers streamed into the streets.
People were cheering and crying and running to the tanks
to hug the heroes who'd brought candy and gum and

FREEDOM.

Where there was hiding,
now there was hope.
People could once again live
and learn
and play
and pray

safe from capture.

They tore up their papers
with the pretend names,
free now to be who they always were.

The Jewish identities
erased from those papers,
hidden in their hearts,
could shine
out in the open
once again.

And yet,
since so many lives were lost,
their freedom was shrouded in sadness.

When the war was over,
it was the Nazis' turn to hide.

They tried to conceal their crimes
and make the world forget
who they were
and what they'd done.

But the world
remembers.

VIVE
LA
FRANCE

AUTHOR'S NOTE

As a Jewish journalist with family killed in the Holocaust, some of my most meaningful interviews have been with survivors who know that time is running out to tell their stories. Amid growing reports of anti-Semitism and Holocaust denial, I feel compelled to help shine a light on the stories of suffering, survival, and those who refused to stand by and watch hate happen.

In 1940, the Germans invaded France. They took over the northern part of the country, and then the French government in the southern part of the country began collaborating with the Nazis. So Jewish people living in France became the target of Hitler's "Final Solution": the intent to remove the Jewish race from the face of the earth. As the persecution began, the French Resistance sprang into action—an active underground network of heroes, risking their lives to sabotage the Germans and provide Jewish people with false identity papers, hiding places, and convoys to Spain, Switzerland, and other safe haven countries. French Resistance members learned of Jewish people scheduled to be arrested, and they set about trying to save them.

Judith Geller, a teenager when the war broke out, was one such hero. When I learned that she used a toy duck to smuggle fake identity papers, and that the duck was in the artifacts collection at Yad Vashem, the World Holocaust Remembrance Center in Israel, I knew I wanted to tell this story. Although specific information about Geller's activities with the duck is limited, this book is based on events that I pieced together from researching general operations of the French Resistance, combined with information I received from Yad Vashem about Geller and the resistance group she worked with. Illustrator Amy June Bates found an account written by Geller to her descendants. Geller's quotes in this note are taken from that account.

A Dutch Resistance worker named Frans Gerritsen made the wooden duck, along with other hollowed-out objects such as a bread board, to hide documents. Geller requested the duck specifically, since she was posing as a child social worker. Her request came after she was almost caught carrying false papers. She was able to stash the papers away before the Nazis could see them. But after that, "the situation was more and more difficult," and she knew she needed a way to conceal the documents.

Above and facing page: The actual toy duck, revealing the secret chamber, that Judith Geller used to hide documents. Courtesy Yad Vashem Artifacts Collection. Loaned by Judith (Geller) Marcus, Israel

"I have not been in a concentration camp, but death has brushed against me more than once," Geller wrote, describing her near-misses with Nazis, as well as with French militia members who helped Germans round up the Jews.

So many people were terrified for their lives and had to hide their families in the hopes of escaping capture. Many were forced to make the devastating decision to send only their children into hiding, since children, with their smaller sizes, were easier to smuggle to safety. And here was a toy whose sole purpose was hiding—hiding documents to help counter the danger and save lives.

To me, the duck is a symbol of shining a light on the truth of the war. Surrounded by memories that the Nazis couldn't destroy, it's in a museum that showcases the suffering and strength of the Jewish people who once lived. It's on display with artifacts like prayer books, stained glass windows, and sacred scrolls that were rescued from burning synagogues. It sits alongside diaries, dolls, shoes, and suitcases that belonged to Jewish prisoners and others killed in concentration camps. From a war that sent so many into hiding, during a time of such utter human darkness, these artifacts are now out in the open and online—for the world to see.

After the war, Judith Geller got married and moved to Israel. Her married name became Yehudit (Hebrew for "Judith") Marcus. She had a son and a daughter. One of their toys was the duck that helped their mother become a hero, risking her life to save people she didn't even know. There were so many lives that couldn't be saved, of course, and so many families that were torn apart. Thirty-two members of Judith Geller's family were killed. "For all of us, this wound will never heal," she wrote.

I held the memory of the victims close as I wrote this book. I hope this serves as a tribute to the lives that were lost and a reminder of the suffering as well as a celebration of the lives that were saved and a recognition of the heroism. I will be donating a portion of my royalties from this book to Yad Vashem.

May more and more truths from the Holocaust continue to come out of the darkness and into the light.

ARTIST'S NOTE

"My name is Judith."

This is how Judith Geller began her account of the five years from 1939–1945. She lived through the war with several pseudonyms, notably Jacqueline Gauthier, in order to hide her Jewish identity, take care of her family in hiding, and resist the Nazi occupation in France. She lost friends and family, including her brother, to the Nazi regime. I can imagine that the words "My name is Judith" carried with them an assertion of authenticity, relief, pride, and defiance.

During those five years of the war, she worked for the French Resistance by riding her bike all over Paris delivering papers, helping to secretly relocate children to orphanages and monasteries, forging documents, and painting out anti-Semitic graffiti. But she also had a job. She worked in Nazi factories that made munitions and uniforms, secretly sabotaging machinery. But finding food to feed her family was a constant struggle above all of this, trying to make rations for one person stretch for her whole family. She kept her parents hidden for four years and delivered food to her brother and her friend Alfred, who were both in Nazi camps on the outskirts of Paris. She was a true heroine.

As a visual storyteller, I am always trying to gather parts of the story that might be seen and not heard. Here are a few details that I drew from Judith's memoir at family-heritage-art. co.il/JudithMarkus/Ceci-est-mon-histoire/Ceci-est-mon-histoire.htm:

Her coat: Judith described the coat that she wears as "a big coat which had been sewn in a military cloth and dyed brown." One story that she told in her memoir is how she and two friends climbed to the top of Sacre-Coeur and threw leaflets that said "Long live France, down with the occupier; France will win." As

Judith Geller's false papers, identifying her as Jacqueline Gauthier. Courtesy Yad Vashem Artifacts Collection. Loaned by Judith (Geller) Marcus, Israel

they were running away, they were taken by the police. Judith's big coat got caught in the door of the police car and the door didn't close properly. As they rounded a corner, her friend pushed her out of the door onto the street, and Judith was able to escape. She never saw her friend again and had leg injuries after the incident for the next two years.

Her bike: The bike was Judith's most valuable possession. Jewish people were not allowed to own bikes or ride on trains. In order to protect her family and work for the resistance, Judith needed the bike and a fake identity to get around. She rode many, many kilometers every day getting food to the people she loved, as well as doing her many jobs, day and night. According to her memoir, once she rode seventy kilometers (forty-three miles) in twenty hours. Helping the Resistance and taking care of her family were her all-consuming priorities. She slept very little.

"Today you will certainly find it foolish to risk your life.
But at that time, everything, every little rebellion was important."
—Judith Geller

AUTHOR'S BIBLIOGRAPHY

WEBSITES

Yad Vashem: The World Holocaust Remembrance Center. "Wooden Duck Used by the French Underground for Smuggling Documents." See yadvashem.org/artifacts/museum/wooden-duck.html.

TESTIMONIES

Marcus, Judith. "Ceci est mon histoire . . ." *The Family Site.* July 1999. See: family-heritage-art.co.il/JudithMarkus/Ceci-est-mon-histoire/Ceci-est-mon-histoire.htm.

INTERVIEWS

Staff at Yad Vashem: The World Holocaust Remembrance Center, email and telephone correspondence. January 2019.

ARTICLES

Radin, Charles A. "From darkness of Holocaust, to light." *Boston Globe*, March 27, 2005. See archive.boston.com/news/world/articles/2005/03/27/from_darkness_of_holocaust_to_light.

BOOKS

Cobb, Matthew. *The Resistance: The French Fight Against the Nazis.* London: Simon & Schuster, 2013.

Gildea, Robert. *Fighters in the Shadows: A New History of the French Resistance.* Cambridge, MA: Belknap Press, 2015.

Rosbottom, Ronald C. *When Paris Went Dark: The City of Light Under German Occupation, 1940–1944.* New York: Back Bay Books, 2015.

The illustrations for this book were made with watercolor,
gouache, and pencil and watercolor paper.

Cataloging-in-Publication Data has been applied for and
may be obtained from the Library of Congress.

ISBN 978-1-4197-5000-7

Text © 2023 Elisa Boxer
Illustrations © 2023 Amy June Bates
Edited by Howard W. Reeves
Book design by Heather Kelly and Natalie Padberg Bartoo

Printed and bound in China
10 9 8 7 6 5 4 3 2

ABRAMS The Art of Books
195 Broadway, New York, NY 10007
abramsbooks.com